Frogs and toads are amphibians (/amfibeeɛnz/). All amphibians like moist places, but they can live on land as well as in ponds and streams. Frogs are different from toads, but they look alike. Can you tell the difference between a frog and a toad?

frog

toad

Frogs have smooth skin but toads have lots of lumps and bumps on them.

a toad with lumpy, bumpy skin

jumping frog

Frogs are good at jumping, while toads take short hops or run along the ground.

Frogs and toads live in ponds, rivers, rainforests and trees!

a frog in a rainforest tree

a frog in a pond

Like frogs, toads need to live where it is moist and wet, but they spend more time on land than frogs do.

a Goliath (/goɑlieeth/) frog

a gray treefrog

Frogs and toads come in all shapes and sizes. Some are so small that they could sit on your fingernail, while the Goliath frog can grow to be 33cm long!

Frogs and toads live in every continent except Antarctica. They do not always avoid the cold, however. Some frogs live within the Arctic circle. The Alaskan wood frog can even survive being frozen in winter. When the thaw comes in spring, the Alaskan wood frog thaws out, too, and hops away to enjoy the summer weather!

Alaskan wood frog

Frogs and toads will catch insects, slugs, snails and spiders. Some larger frogs catch lizards, snakes and small birds. The frogs wait for an animal to come to them, and then... gulp! They gobble it down whole.

a strawberry poison dart frog

Frogs have a lot of predators: herons, snakes, fish, otters, birds and hedgehogs all eat frogs.

heron

frog

Frogs and toads shed their skin as they grow.

Toads have fewer predators because their skin is bitter and not nice to eat. Toad skin can also smell a bit like a skunk!

Poison dart frogs live in Central and South America. They are extremely poisonous. Their bright markings alert other animals to the fact that they are toxic.

poison dart frog

Hunters from the tribes that live in the rainforest use the poison from these frogs. They dip the points of their arrows in it. The poison will paralyse an animal, or make it vomit or swell up.

Hunters have to be careful with the frog's poison, or it will kill them as well.

arrow

golden poison arrow frog

In spring, male frogs and toads croak to attract a mate. All frogs and toads need a pond to lay their eggs in. The female lays eggs called spawn.

frogspawn

The black dot is the developing frog or toad. It is surrounded by layers of jelly that help to protect it and keep it afloat.

Frogspawn floats in big clumps. There might be several thousand eggs in a clump.

frogspawn

jelly

a developing frog

Toad spawn is laid in long chains.

toad spawn

A few days after being laid, the eggs hatch into tadpoles.

egg developing frog tadpole

A few weeks after that, the tadpoles grow legs. The back legs grow first. After a while, their tails start to shrink and the tadpoles begin to look more like frogs.

tadpole

tail

back leg

front leg

They are now froglets. When they develop lungs and can breathe air, they hop out of the pond and onto the land.

froglet

adult frog

When an animal changes shape like this it is called metamorphosis (/me-tɛ-**mor**-fɛ-sis/).

Despite its name, the Surinam toad is really a type of frog! It is called a toad because of its lumpy-looking skin. It lives on muddy riverbeds in the rainforest, where it floats about looking like a dead leaf.

Surinam toad

When Surinam toads mate, the male guides the eggs to the female's back where they stick.

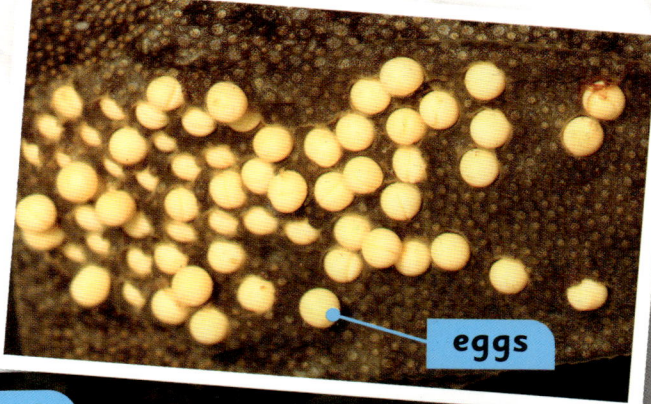

eggs

female Surinam toad

skin growing around eggs

The skin grows around the eggs until you cannot see them. They continue to develop under the skin. When they are ready, the pockets in the skin open up and the little froglets emerge.

Unlikely as it sounds, some frogs can fly! The Malabar flying frog lives in the canopy of the rainforest, and uses its webbed feet like sails to fly — or glide — from tree to tree or to the ground.

Sticky discs help the frog to land and grip onto vertical surfaces.